MW00815302

The LOUISIANA PURCHASE

MORE ADVANCE PRAISE FOR
The LOUISIANA PURCHASE

"Gracefully athletic and soulfully centered, *The Louisiana Purchase* slides into us bearing an olive branch as its red bird Brock. Always open, "never locked," Goar's season on earth contains all the wisdom of the ancient almanacs of the future; a unique, private cosmology founded on the soundest of poetic principles: conservation of what matters. *The Louisiana Purchase* signals a renewed project in poetry: to seek, perchance to find what is holy, and if not, make it so. This book is an instrument for being."

—*Loren Goodman, author of* Famous Americans

"With America behaving as it does today, we all need to better understand the American beauty of years past and the American beauty that is yet to come. Jim Goar's *The Louisiana Purchase* reinvents a landscape so similar and dissimilar to what we know of a country's terrain that it is obviously a beauty that is yet to be. Or more so, Goar reinvents a country that has no limits because it exists in the alternate space of the supernatural. So that a "President's signature is printed on the face of the moon" in order to create a world where "Kansas starts to bleed" so that "the sun is taken from the sky" and likewise, to make a space where a human-modified moon can exist with us in a plain way, do our bidding, and also fight back. You should read this book. It's not the American story you learned about in third grade. It's the one you wanted to learn. It's the one that was always the true story."

—*Dorothea Lasky, author of* Black Life

Also by Jim Goar

Seoul Bus Poems

The LOUISIANA PURCHASE

Jim Goar

Gina,
finally! In Person!

Jim
15 April 2012

Rose Metal Press

Copyright © 2011 by Jim Goar

All rights reserved. No part of this book may be used or reproduced in any manner
without written permission from the publisher except in case of brief quotations
within critical articles and reviews.

Rose Metal Press, Inc.
P.O. Box 1956
Brookline, MA 02446
rosemetalpress@gmail.com
www.rosemetalpress.com

Library of Congress Control Number: 2011941321

ISBN: 978-0-9846166-3-3

Cover and interior design by Heather Butterfield
See "A Note About the Type" on page 81 for more information about the typefaces used.

Cover art: *The Rower*, by Fran Forman
More information and artwork can be viewed on the artist's website: www.franforman.com.

This book is manufactured in the United States of America and printed on acid-free paper.

For Sang-yeon

ACKNOWLEDGMENTS

I'd like to thank Pirooz Kalayeh for working over, talking through, and helping me find order in *The Louisiana Purchase*. I'd also like to thank Scott Pierce, whose effing press published a swath of *The Louisiana Purchase* as the chapbook *Whole Milk*. Many thanks to the editors of the following journals where some of these pieces originally appeared: *Bullfight, Country Music, elimae, Ellipses, Nidus, So and So*, and *Three Therefore Two*. And, of course, thank you to the editors of Rose Metal Press, Abigail Beckel and Kathleen Rooney, who have helped to make *The Louisiana Purchase* what it is today.

AUTHOR'S NOTE

Though he'd acquired roughly 828,000 square miles for the United States, President Thomas Jefferson was unsure what the newly bought territory contained, as well as how far west it extended. To remedy this lack, he sent out an expedition headed by Meriwether Lewis and William Clark, the latter being a cartographer.

They set off from just outside St. Louis, Missouri in 1804, and—after encountering some 50 tribes and "discovering" 300 "new" plants and animals—returned in 1806. For the next thirty years, Clark's map was the most detailed rendering of the Louisiana Purchase.

A century and a half later, a map of the United States is unspooled. Much of the heartland is covered by a green fog that stretches from the

Mississippi River to the eastern edge of Idaho. The teacher begins a lesson: Led by two veterans of the Indian Wars, the Corps of Discovery journeyed into the Louisiana Purchase.

Some books are written about an external subject; what follows is a different kind of book. The gathered pieces of *The Louisiana Purchase* do not attempt to describe anything beyond their borders and instead use the Louisiana Purchase, with its impossible vastness and mythical promise, as a framework in which a new exploration can occur. By dislodging historical and personal terms—and allowing them to interweave and settle into unfamiliar contexts—the grouping of these pieces becomes a territory in and of itself. *The Louisiana Purchase* is the mapping of its own ongoing and haphazard occurrence, not a representation or recounting of the past event or its subsequent exploration.

Assembled from fractured myths, Westerns, Disney, fictions, childhood memories, life abroad, and primary sources, what follows is my uneven, transitioning, and forever incomplete America. *The Louisiana Purchase*, an attempt to locate what I contain, is both the expedition as well as its report.

—*Jim Goar*

THE LOUISIANA PURCHASE

*The object of your mission is to explore
the Missouri River and its communications with
the waters of the Pacific*

— President Thomas Jefferson

This book contains all of Arkansas, Missouri, Iowa 1806, Oklahoma, Kansas, Nebraska, Minnesota south of the Mississippi River, much of North Dakota, nearly all of South Dakota, northeastern New Mexico, northern Texas, the portions of Montana, Wyoming, and Colorado east of the Continental Divide, and Louisiana on both sides of the Mississippi River, including the city of New Orleans.

1803 United States acquires Iowa 1806 in the Louisiana
Purchase.

1806

May 14, 1804 *We have begun an expedition*
westward into the interior parts
of the Louisiana Purchase

Clark's map is tied by a yellow ribbon. I untie it and the map rolls flat on the table. I climb onto the table and fall into Iowa 1806. No need to make more of it. Welcome to Iowa 1806. Your gun is over the door. Your eggs, over easy. The dust like a good boy slaps his girl and Missouri gets buried.

President Jefferson walks off the mound. The
Cardinals take the field. Ozzie Smith falls over dead.
The crowd falls silent. Phil Niekro throws a ball at
the sky. The ball does not return. We call it the
moon. It becomes a crescent. When Jefferson holds
up two fingers, the moon breaks into the dirt.

The President's signature is printed on the face of
the moon. The moon is returned to the sky. A few
days pass before the moon's rotations cease. An
expert is summoned. Her explanation is brief: "The
moon has been doctored." Effigies of Niekro are
burned. There is a run on canned goods. We hide in
our cellars and await the tide.

The moon arrives in a pair of red shoes. Iowa 1806
looks good in shade. I invite them into my home. The
moon barely fits. Jefferson pokes fun: "Crescent
Moon, she's going to kill you." And the moon, a vessel
of suns—something you can't move—bites off the
lower half of Texas.

The moon is tied to Iowa 1806 by a yellow ribbon. They rise and set inside my house. By the end of the month the moon has grown too big. Jefferson orders me to cut it loose. His demand is leaked to the public. The public does not object. Since there are no voices of dissent, I carry out the president's wish. Iowa 1806 collapses; the moon just disappears.

It is December and Iowa
1806 does not look good.

On the eve of the election, Kansas starts to bleed. Jefferson suspects the moon. The Pinkertons investigate the heavens. Constellations are upturned. When the moon cannot be found, the sun is taken from the sky.

Thirty days of night begin. Vampires come out of the woodwork. Blood and tears flow. The ex-jock fights back. A vampire is decapitated. Some popcorn lands on my head. I hear a woman's voice and turn around. The moon is sitting at her side.

Mrs. Jefferson is carrying a torch for the moon to see. The President attempts to extinguish her flame. Martha tells him to sleep on the couch. He tells her he will, but that night he sleeps under the stars instead.

Snow falls on Iowa 1806. Roads and schools are closed. The winter blues move in. The snow does not abate. Christmas is cancelled. Jefferson washes his hands and takes to the rails. Iowa 1806 falls into a great depression.

In wet weather, plant seeds only an inch deep, so the seeds won't rot. Otherwise, plant them at least two inches deep, especially for late plantings in warm or dry weather, when it is important to keep them moist. The deeper the seeds are, the harder it is for the cardinals to find them.

Eight cardinals fly over Iowa 1806. I give them shelter.
They leave nothing but their droppings. The gestation
period is short. Iowa 1806 blossoms. The father is not
in doubt; hundreds of crying moons disturb the sky.

1673 French explorers Louis Jolliet and Father
Marquette canoe up the Arkansas River and into
the mouth of Iowa 1806.

The Vatican sees a crescent shining through the clouds of Rome. Emissaries are sent. Marquette and Jolliet arrive at my door. Iowa 1806 makes them feel at home. They have forgotten their gifts—so I forget mine. A scuffle ensues.

The moon is over Lake Itasca.
"Lake Itasca, Lake Itasca"
The moon is over Lake Itasca.

The new moon floats on Lake
Itasca. And waits in Lake Itasca.
And drinks from Lake Itasca.

The moon grows fat in Lake
Itasca. Eats pizza with Lake Itasca.
Drinks Masi with Lake Itasca.
Leaves Lake Itasca for the sky.

The moon is over Lake Itasca

"Lake Itasca, Lake Itasca"

The moon is over Lake Itasca.

I shake my left fist at the moon. The moon returns in kind. I shake my right fist at the moon. The moon returns in kind. I shake a white fish at the moon. The moon returns in kind. I gesticulate at the moon. The moon returns in kind. I throw Iowa 1806 at the moon. The moon returns in kind. I sleep under a blanket of Iowa 1806. The moon never sleeps.

Iowa 1806 is overrun by Iowa
1807. Nothing much changes.

If you keep your door shut, the moon will not come
in. No need to make more of it. Welcome to Iowa
1807. Your gun is on the floor. Your eggs, over
easy. The dusk like a good boy slaps his girl and
Kansas gets buried.

May 14, 1805 Radio is introduced to Iowa 1806.

THE CORPS OF DISCOVERY

May 17, 1805 We begin to encounter animals
we'd never before seen, and,
following President Jefferson's
instructions, take measure of
the new species.

The Red-Faced Bird

Iowa 1806 wanted to be free as radio.
Secession seemed the only option.
In this way the matter was resolved:
"Iowa, you'll no longer see radio, you won't."

A tree sprouted from my penis. The red-faced bird came to nest. When I found auburn leaves on my sheets I encouraged the bird to go. It claimed squatters' rights. I called the police. They summoned a lumberjack. This was not the outcome either of us desired. Now the red-faced bird visits on Tuesdays and Thursdays.

I'm barbecuing in the snow. The red-faced bird is watching me intently. I get the feeling that I'm late. I put some honey on the moon. I offer the bird a Keystone. It accepts and drinks it quick. I've forgotten how to serve a moon and ask the bird. It flies away. Worthless drunk. The moon begins to burn. I begin to panic. I try to remove it. It falls through my spatula and into the fire. I feel I've committed a great sin.

The law has relocated the entire population.
Hill people now live in valleys. Those by the ocean
now live in the desert. Everyone has moved to their
opposite location. In this way communities stay
intact.

A tree sprouted from my penis. The red-faced bird came to nest. When I found auburn leaves on my sheets I encouraged the bird to go. It claimed squatters' rights. I called the police. They summoned a lumberjack. This was not the outcome either of us desired. Now the red-faced bird visits on Tuesdays and Sundays.

An elephant crawls under my house. Floor boards creak. Water lines burst. All dry land is soon gone. For eleven months, I await the plumber. Just when I think I've been forgotten, the red-faced bird arrives. It's come to borrow a pinch of thyme. I ask it for some help. It tells me to use a wrench. I do. The flooding stops. I open my cabinet. All the thyme is gone. I give the bird an olive instead.

September 20, 1806 We went out that day and saw a herd of elephant covering the prairie and endeavored to capture one for transport east to President Jefferson.

The Elephant

Iowa 1806 needed two million nine hundred twenty-three thousand one hundred seventy-nine Big Macs and a Diet Coke.

"What size?"

"Medium. Large," I look to Iowa 1806. "No, medium."

"Will that be all?"

"Uh-huh."

"Please pull up to the first window."

When I learn that *Dumbo* is showing again I know there will be problems. I warn the elephant. It pays no heed and sees the flick. Two days later it builds a nest. My neighbors complain. I bake them cookies. They call the law. The law has an idea: *Eight fire-eating midgets and a sad clown will persuade the elephant to join the circus.* For twenty-two days they try. The elephant is not swayed. I am. The clown says OK. But the midgets don't think I'm circus material.

"You, elephant, move on!"
It does not move, so I do. I settle into another hammock.
The view is nice between my socks. I go to sleep. I wake.
The elephant is there between my socks. I make
horrendous faces at it. It does not move. I cover it in mud.
When the tide goes out, I can see its feet.

I leave my eyes open and face the turned off TV. Beside it is the front door. The wind opens the door. A girl rides her bike on the sidewalk. Two red leaves fall into her basket. Her scarf has tassels and her hat a red ball which follows behind. The front wheel of her bike disengages and rolls into the street. A red convertible hits the tire. It bounces through my open door and makes itself at home.

"Have you any eggs?" it asks.

"Unfortunately, I don't."

It turns on the Radio and we listen to the World Series.

The telegram arrives at my door. It sings a little ditty about my eviction. I take the news well and give it a dollar. It tips its hat and says, "Good day." I leave my home at once.

I am riding on the back of the elephant. It pays no attention to traffic lights. Soon the police are involved. We are cuffed and thrown in the back of a cruiser. The elephant begins to cry. Within seconds the car is filled with tears. The law rolls down the windows so it can breathe. We take this opportunity to escape.

November 2, 1806   As the days shorten, our thoughts turn to home.

An Honest Woman

"Please come home, Pumpkin. You left a hole the size of Iowa 1806 when you left, you did."

A gunfight has just concluded. Eight corpses will not be moved. "Buzzards and worms both got to eat," a child says. "In this town no one is buried."

An honest woman comes out of the bank. Dollar
signs are printed on the bags she carries. I ask her
for some change. She offers work. I suggest lunch.
She says I'll get what I want if I follow her home.

I open the refrigerator door. There is only one hot dog left. I cut it in two. It is filled with leaves. She says this is common. When I hesitate, she eats both halves.

In parting she gives me her arm.
This feels a bit dramatic, so I hide
it under my coat.

November 17, 1806 Negotiated a purchase of the horses our men will need to arrive at the other side of the mountains.

My Horse & The Pianist

Iowa 1806's neighbors were on edge.

The pianist tells another joke. The crowd laughs. I
don't. I raise my hand. An usher leads me to the
stage. I tell the pianist that I've come to dance. She
draws a six-shooter and fires at my boots.

"Why surrender when you're not wanted?" My horse looks at me with sad eyes and turns itself in. I petition the law. My petition is denied: *the law does not allow take backs.* My horse is blindfolded and given a cigarette. Its stoicism inspires the crowd. They demand proof of a broken leg. When none is given they liberate my horse. For the next eight days, it is the symbol of their revolution.

A reporter is sent to cover the eight-day revolution. My horse wears a Richard Nixon mask to the interview. "Are you funded by communists?" My horse remains silent. The reporter searches in a coat pocket. "Some sugar perhaps?" My horse eats three sugar cubes out of the reporter's hand. A flash goes off. Two days later this photo appears in the *Arizona Daily Star*.

The law wears a black paper hat and shoes with large
buckles. It serves us turkey then pumpkin pie. When
we are done it leaves the room. We wait. The law
does not return. I ask her if she knows where it went.
She points to the chimney. It crawls out dressed as
Saint Nick. I apologize for overstaying our welcome.
It tells me not to worry, then gives us a jug of whiskey
and two dirty blankets.

The law wishes to finish what it started. My horse is blindfolded and given a cigarette. A firing squad awaits the order. Before it can be given, my horse falls over dead.

She takes the urn off the mantle. We mix
his ashes with plastic. The resulting frisbee
is orange. We throw it around the yard.
Eventually it lands on the roof.

THE NORTHWEST PASSAGE

September 23, 1807 *After six months of arduous*
travel we arrive at the last point
of our map, beyond which,
everything is only rumor and
conjecture.

April 13, 1743 –
July 4, 1826
President Jefferson has a mind that encompasses the Louisiana Purchase.

The Louisiana Purchase is kept in a glass box so it will remain, now and forever, empty. We are not allowed to take pictures, nor get closer than ten yards.

At three o'clock every day (except for holidays, when it is not displayed at all), the Service Man exits his room, lifts The Louisiana Purchase off the mantle, puts it into a shoebox (He carries it in a shoebox! In a shoebox, you must understand.), walks back to his room, utters a mantra, and closes the door.

Though (in moments of weakness) we've begged, he will not tell us his name, nor will he show us his face which we imagine to be hideous. (Why else would he wear a mask?) The only response he gives our cries of anguish—and in reality, our cries of anguish are a response to it—is a mantra that I cannot hear without tearing at my gentle flesh.

Sometimes we are foolish enough to hope that he will enter his room without speaking it. These hopes have never been realized. Instead, each and every time, he stops at the precipice of his dwelling as though he forgot and remembered something. There he clears his throat (Mind you, his back is to us. He does not turn around. Even that small pittance of respect he will not give.), then utters a mantra we must strain to hear: "A flower too often smelt will wilt."

Once, years ago, I shouted back, "But how can we smell The Purchase through your savage breath?" His laughter was so demonic that we now allow his mantra to linger in the air without rebuttal until he closes the door behind him.

Then we wail.

Two blue eyes, one from cataracts, the other from birth, were the last of my possessions they took. So you see, I've never laid eyes on the man who walks with the awkward pace of an atrophied leg along the corridor outside my cell.

For such an insignificant, it seems absurd, but I am the only charge of this guard, and he must be a guard and not a prisoner, for what kind of an architect builds a door which leads only to another cell.

Though awkward, his pace is consistent, and has yet to stop, it only turns; and it only turns to retrace the steps of a myriad journey already made, from wall to wall, in front of my cell, before it turns again.

Since he is the only guard to walk outside my cell, and I am his only prisoner, it stands to reason that my release would also be his; and since my release is impossible, his reprieve is at best improbable.

I cannot help but shudder at the thought of a man who would take on such a commission.

After supplication before The Louisiana Purchase and before descent back into town, it is only the most pious, the blind and the penitent who do not stand to look. There are no seams where the wood bisects to make this holy symbol. Two limbs appear to branch from the stem at right angles. So organic does The Purchase look that pilgrims, after their first descent, ask priests if it does not simply grow from the mountain. The holy men reply that the lotus does grow from the filthiest of waters; that the rock from which The Purchase springs was not always red. They say ancients sacrificed animals there, their enemies, then themselves, until there were no more; that The Purchase, germinated in blood, grew prior to the Immaculate Conception; that it portended the deity; that the symbol came first.

The poor dine in air-conditioned mansions (away from the heat of the desert). Between the hours of three and five, while the day is still hot, they gather to perform calisthenics and review their military training. When these chores are done, it is off to parties, where women, dressed in beautiful gowns, raise toasts to the chivalry of their men, and their men, in tuxedos of the latest French cut, discuss the looming war.

The rich, on the other hand, take their meals in heated restaurants. When a customer enters, he removes his gray shirt and hangs it next to the others. He sits at the table with eight other sweaty men and serves himself from the communal bowl of glutinous rice and chili peppers. He washes the meal down with scalding tea that tastes like grass.

When the steam whistle blows, he returns to a factory, or construction yard, or to digging ditches. At four o'clock, when the whistle blows again, he puts down his shovel or axe, takes a shower, and hurries off to his position in the government.

At first these habits might seem curious, but after speaking with the townspeople for a short while, they begin to make sense.

The rich organized the society and have the power to change it; they control the money and the government, are organized and well-educated. In fact, it is their education which makes this society possible. In their studies, they were taught, and have learned, that by living as they do, they ensure the greatness of their state.

The poor, though less concerned with the greatness of their state, love the lifestyle it affords and are painfully aware that no other state, constructed as theirs, exists. And so, when a foreign power threatens, the poor eagerly meet them in battle; and with garbage men and sewage workers commanding the military from afar, they inevitably triumph, though often at great cost.

The Louisiana Purchase, so long denied, then contained, and finally eradicated, had trickled in, past the outer wall, and even the isolation of the first patients I'd seen with the telltale signs, the tower guards, was not enough to quell its spread.

The moment I said "epidemic" to the king's advisor, I became undesirable, and to ensure I'd not arouse panic in those more easily swayed, he did me a great favor, and placed me in a cell with full rations and no windows so that no more than our four ears could hear my dangerous prognosis.

My release, when it came, was not proclaimed; instead it was declared on a note I found outside my cell, and, considering my door was never locked, the declaration, signed by the king's advisor, was an altruistic gesture that rang a bit hollow.

From his note I discerned that not only was I the last physician, but also the last citizen who was not a patient, or, more accurately, would have been a patient had there been doctors left to perform their duties.

Because I'd obeyed my edict of incarceration, I adhered to this unfortunate pardon and emerged from my cell onto an empty street, across from which, hung from a second story balcony, The Louisiana Purchase had begun to rot.

The tone is heard every dusk and twice at dawn, and every dusk and twice at dawn, the birds arrive to perch upon our town and flesh. Though house and head alike collapse, the shingles of a roof can be replaced; a crown of silken hair cannot. Last week, from the kitchen window, I saw the neighbor child, arms outstretched, fold beneath the din of hawks. And after a moment's pause, in the unfurling of wings, I watched his lifeless body flown beyond our highest kite.

The shadow whole of the moon, visible behind an ardent crescent, lured me outside where I knelt on the retracted flowers of The Louisiana Purchase. I took The Purchase in my fingers and sublimated it with little twists—then bigger twists and circular tugs—until the roots began to slip from the dirt.

1682   LaSalle explored the Mississippi River from its mouth and claimed the river and all land drained by it for Louis XIV, the King of France.

Now it is only the queen who appears on the balcony. She looks out over her subjects, gathered in the ancient square, and with a smile, recounts how a century before, her husband's family, in one bloody night, retook the throne.

The crowd knows its part, and weeps when it should, shouts when it should, and howls "No" or "Yes" as one, then falls silent and waits until it is needed again.

Her tale complete, the queen raises her cup, turns it over, to show that she, like us, has nothing left, and we, caught off guard, without a cup to raise, begin to sing a ballad first heard a century before by our men, camped outside these walls, anticipating gold and the pleasure of dark-skinned women.

Iowa 1806 sits on a rocky bluff. The rocks are smooth and black and when dampened by the ocean they shine like glass. Gray concrete walls rise from these black rocks and barbed wire hangs over them. Soldiers stand on these walls and watch the sky and the ocean and the people who walk in the courtyard three stories below. The people walk on cobblestones which lead to stairs which lead down to the pool where you can buy a beer at seven o'clock in the morning. And in the morning, with only The Louisiana Purchase for company, one need not listen to hear the ocean.

Midgets are revered by the people who live at the mountain's base for they most resemble the ancients. A narrow path cut into the mountain's face supports the peoples' belief that the ancients were small. Only the diminutive can traverse this path as bipeds; all others must propel themselves as beasts.

In the past, academics hypothesized that the ancients were no different in stature than those who now exist, and like the people now, also revered the diminutive (though for what reason they could not say). Now it is believed (amongst the learned) that the diminutive were not held in high regard. That the path had nothing to do with them at all. They point to a young archeologist's discovery of tablets on which charcoal-etched, open-mouthed serpents, ascend through the earth by a series of labyrinths. Sadly though, these tablets were misplaced just prior to their first public viewing; but documentary photographs are said to exist.

Another possibility, the one which the priests espouse, is that the ancient builders carved without the knowledge of why, that God's hand was on them, that they were his tools, and the path was not meant for them. It is irrelevant if the people, short or tall, worshipped serpents or dwarfs or Zeus, they say. The pathway was commissioned by God for those who were to come later. God desired the path narrow so the pious could, and in most cases must, ascend the mountain in the most penitent of stances.

A slow procession leads beyond the wall and over sand where, one by one, our aged women shuffle through the surf, then dive into the sea. Because her aged husband can never leave the land, and she will only once more leave the sea, she sits at the table with her back against the swells, while he faces the salt and the sharks just beyond the beach.

Words burrowed into The Louisiana Purchase until the underside of letters existed against nothing but themselves and the air, and then the air, without them, continued to exist.

A NOTE ABOUT THE TYPE

The main text of *The Louisiana Purchase* is set in Bell. Richard Austin cut the type, an English transitional, for John Bell circa 1788 (fifteen years before the Louisiana Purchase). Bell was an English book and newspaper publisher, and used the font in his paper *The Oracle*. The type design was inspired by French punchcutters of the era who were creating vertical letterforms with extreme contrast between thick and thin—what we now classify as modern. Bell is less severe than modern typefaces, and remains a popular body font with its highly readable roman forms.

There are two display faces used throughout this book: Perpetua Titling and P22 Operina. Perpetua is a transitional English type designed by Eric Gill and released in 1929. Stanley Morison described Perpetua as having a "noble, monumental, appearance" in large sizes, which perhaps reflects Gill's background as a sculptor. P22 Operina is a revival based on the handwriting of sixteenth-century Italian scribe Ludovico degli Arrighi. Released in 2003, Operina has a charming historic quality with its elaborate shapes and rough texture.

—*Heather Butterfield*